APPRENTICESHIP PROGRAM FOR MOS OF
CENTRAL OFFICE REPAIRER

WORK EXPERIENCE LOG

APPRENTICE NAME

DEPARTMENT OF THE NAVY
HEADQUARTERS OF THE UNITED STATES MARINE CORPS
WASHINGTON, D.C. 20380

TABLE OF CONTENTS

INTRODUCTION

APPRENTICESHIP

Apprenticeship is training for jobs in technical trades that require special skills and knowledge. It involves technical schooling and planned on-the-job training under supervision. For young workers desiring to gain a skilled occupation, the apprenticeship program provides a step by step program of instruction and on-the-job training. This program will lead to advanced standing in the technical skill or trade you have chosen.

The USMC Apprenticeship Program provides you with the opportunity to meet some requirements for advancement in your chosen skill area while on active duty. As you progress in your training in the Marine Corps and master the skills required of your trade, you will have the mastered skills recorded in your log. Our apprenticeship program allows you to make your work experience in the Marine Corps count twice. First, to fulfill your active duty obligation in a productive manner. Second, to provide you with a usable skill if you should decide to return to civilian life. By having documented proof of Marine Corps schooling and work experience, you should qualify for a better job at higher pay.

Most apprenticeship terms range from 1 to 4 year, depending upon the trade involved. To master a particular trade requires: (1) Learning all or most of the skills of the trade; (2) Perfecting each specific skill; (3) Bringing each skill up to the speed and accuracy required of the job; and (4) Learning to use specific skills in combination with other skills.

MARINE CORPS APPRENTICESHIP PROGRAM

The purpose of establishing the Marine Corps Apprenticeship Program is to provide Marine Corps commanders an opportunity to implement programs of apprenticeship for military personnel in occupations closely related and applicable to private industry needs and requirements. Marine Corps school training and experience in the field will, if properly documented, satisfy private industry requirements for the training of apprentices in nationally recognized apprenticeable occupations.

The ultimate objective of the United States Marine Corps Apprenticeship Program is to provide registered certification of an individual Marine's skilled craft occupational training. The program has been designed to achieve recognition for Marines equal to their civilian counterparts.

Registration of the National Apprenticeships standards for the United States Marine Corps with the Bureau of Apprenticeship and Training, U.S. Department of Labor, is beneficial to the Marine Corps, to individual Marines, and to private industry, management, and labor. Acceptance of U.S. Marine Corps apprentices as skilled craft-workers by private industry, management, and labor will enhance Marines' employment opportunities as veterans, shorten the term of private industry apprenticeship through the award of appropriate credit for previous military training experience, and provided a source of registered skilled personnel to meet national manpower requirements.

THE CENTRAL OFFICE REPAIRER APPRENTICESHIP PROGRAM

The purpose of this pamphlet is to announce the United States Marine Corps Apprenticeship Program for the trade of Central Office Repairer.

Policies and procedures for participation in the program are contained in MCO 1550.22.

Marines holding a primary or secondary 2811 2818, 2827, 2829 MOS and who are serving in that MOS may participate in the program.

This is an 8000 hour program which leads to a certification of journeyman in the trade of Central Office Repairer by the U.S. Department of Labor. Participation in the program is voluntary and no membership in labor unions or professional associations is required. The work process schedule and schedule of related instruction are outlined on pages 8 through 12. The purpose of the work process schedule and the schedule of related instruction is as indicated below:

> The work process schedule reflects categories of work experience required by Marine apprentices to qualify as Journeyman Central Office Repairer.

> The schedule of related instruction identifies courses which are available to Marine apprentices to satisfy the 1414 hours of annual related instruction required for completion of the program.

Marines eligible for the program may enroll by contacting the Unit or Base Education Officer who will assist in the preparation of the application.

Apprentice logs and instructions on their use will be provided by the Education Officer at the time of registration. Marine apprentices will be required to maintain their log sheets on a <u>daily</u> basis. Log entries must be verified by the Marine apprentice's immediate supervisor on a <u>weekly</u> basis.

Marines who have partially completed an approved Federal or State registered civilian apprenticeship will be awarded credit within the constraints of the individual apprenticeship training program standards. Each training hour successfully completed in the occupation involved will be awarded credit upon presentation of authenticated documentation. Marines serving beyond their initial enlistment are considered career Marines, and may make application for the apprenticeship program in order to be certified as having completed an apprentice program. Career Marine apprentices must complete the same requirements as the first-term apprentice except that they will be given credit for one-half the hours required for the specific apprenticeship program in which they are enrolled provided their previous enlistment was served in an MOS applicable to the relevant apprenticeship program for which applying.

Organized related instruction for all United States Marine Corps apprentices will be defined by the individual apprenticeship program standards. Such related instruction will be provided on an hour-per-year basis, or the total hours my be achieved through the successful completion of a multi-week training course for the apprenticeable occupation involved at any United States Marine Corps training school, or other Service School (Army, Navy, etc.) providing such training

Upon successful completion of apprenticeship training and experience requirements as prescribed by individual apprenticeship program standards, the apprentice will submit a request via the chain of command, accompanied by a letter from the appropriate commander or education officer, to the Office of National Industry Promotion, Bureau of Apprenticeship and Training, U.S. Department of labor, Washington, D.C. 20213, for issuance of a Certificate of Completion of Apprenticeship (Enclosure 10). The Bureau of Apprenticeship and Training will issue all Certificates of Completion of Apprenticeship to the individual through Headquarters, U.S. Marine Corps (Code OTTE) to the appropriate commander.

NATIONAL APPRENTICESHIP STANDARDS

FOR

THE UNITED STATES MARINE CORPS

Developed by Headquarters United States
Marine Corps, Washington, D.C., with the
assistance of the Bureau of Apprenticeship
and Training, Employment and Training
Administration, United States Department
of Labor, Washington, D.C.

AUTHORITY

National Apprenticeship Standards for the United States
Marine Corps are established by authority of:

W. GRAHAM CLAYTOR JR.
Secretary of the Navy

RAY MARSHALL
Secretary, United States
Department of Labor

LOUIS H. WILSON
Commandant of the
Marine Corps

Registered as incorporating the basic standards
recommended by the Bureau of Apprenticeship and
Training, Employment and Training Administration,
United States Department of Labor.

HUGH C. MURPHY
Administrator
Bureau of Apprenticeship and Training
Employment and Training Administration

Registration Number: N-91040   Date: July 7, 1977

DEFINITIONS

1. EMPLOYER---------------The United States Marine Corps9
2. PROGRAM SUPERVISOR-----Commanding General
                          Communication-Electronic School
                          Marine Corps Air Ground Combat Center
                          29 Palms, California 92278
3. NATIONAL APPRENTICESHIP
    STANDARDS--------------The entire document which embodies
                          the procedures for the selection
                          and training of Marine Corps appren-
                          tices and sets forth all the con-
                          ditions associated therewith, in-
                          cluding training on the job, relat-
                          ed technical instruction, and ad-
                          ministrative responsibilities.
4. WORK EXPERIENCE LOG----A book issued to each registered
                          apprentice identifying the occu-
                          pation, work process training
                          schedule, hours allocated to each
                          training task increment in the
                          work process schedule, and sup-
                          ervisory certification require-
                          ments.
5. APPRENTICE-------------Any individual who is on active
                          duty in the U.S. Marine Corps,
                          meets entry age requirements,
                          performs assignments that include
                          training In an apprenticeable
                          occupation and who is registered
                          with the Bureau of Apprenticeship
                          and Training, U.S. Department of
                          Labor, Washington, D.C..
6. REGISTRATION AGENCY----The Bureau or Apprenticeship and
                          Training, U.S. Department of
                          Labor, Washington, D.C..
7. WORK PROCESS SCHEDULE---An outline or work procedures
                          which specifies the required
                          supervised work experience,
                          training on the job, and the
                          approximate time to be spent in
                          each major process.

8. SCHEDULE OF RELATED INSTRUCTION --- Organized, related and supple-
                                         mental instruction necessary to
                                         provide apprentices with knowl-
                                         edge in technical subjects related
                                         to the trade. The instruction may
                                         include supervised correspondence
                                         or self-study courses, as approved
                                         by law or by policy of the regis-
                                         tration agency. A minimum of 144
                                         hours each year of apprenticeship
                                         training is required. It may also
                                         include resident instruction at a
                                         DOD or civilian school. Normally,
                                         a minimum of 144 hours annually
                                         is required. However resident,
                                         formal schooling can satisfy total
                                         requirements for related instruc
                                         tion if over 360 hours are
                                         attained,

1. <u>Participant Designation.</u> Marines working in the military occupational specialties (MOS's)2811, 2818, 2827, or 2829 are authorized to participate in the program.

2. <u>Job Description.</u> As a result of formal training received in conjunction with MOS qualification, participants are knowledge-able in: the functioning of a telephone exchange; assisting an experienced central office repairer; the use and application of systems terminology; assisting with the installation and wiring of distributing frames; safety procedures used in telephone central offices; preparing maintenance forms for dial central office equipment; cleaning and inspecting telephone switching can covers, relay contacts, and terminal blocks; the cleaning, lubrication and inspecting of electrical stepping switches; the skill of aligning dial telephone central office equipment through use of proper procedures, test sets, tools, and manuals to adjust and align: line conditioning equipment, intercept equipment, and autovon trunk circuit equipment; recognizing the significance of the cable color; proper soldering techniques for cable and wires; the techniques of wire wrapping; operating a test desk to determine faults within an outside central office; performing testing procedures using multitesters and oscilloscopes; detecting, identifying, isolating, and finding equipment and line faults; removing and replacing defective parts using a soldering gun and required hand tools; applying relay adjustments; requisitioning repair parts; and applying proper troubleshooting and safety procedures.

Work Experience Functions

CENTRAL OFFICE REPAIRER

(D.O.T. 822.281-041)

Approx hrs.

1. Orientation

   a. Observe functioning of a telephone exchange   500
   b. Assist an experienced dial central office
      repairer.
   c. Develop skills in use and application of
      systems terminology.
   d. Assist central office repairer in instal-
      lation and wiring of distributing frames.
   e. Develop shop cleaning techniques.
   f. Apply safety practices used in telephone
      central offices.

2. Perform Preventive Maintenance of Dial Central   1000
   Office Equipment

   a. Prepare maintenance forms for dial central
      office equipment.

   b. Clean and inspect telephone switching can
      covers, relay contacts, equipment; cables
      and terminal blocks.
   c. Clean, lubricate and inspect electrical
      stepping switches.

3. Develop Skill of Aligning Dial Telephone Central   1000
   Office Equipment through Use of Proper Procedures,
   Test Sets, Tools and Manuals to Adjust and Align:

   a. Line conditioning equipment
   b. Intercept equipment
   c. AUTOVON trunk circuit equipment

4. Install Dial Telephone Central Office Equipment   1000

   a. Observe installation practices and assist
      experienced repairers.
   b. Recognize significance and apply cable color
      codes.
   c. Develop skills in proper soldering techniques
      for cable and wires.
   d. Develop proficiency in the techniques of wire
      wrapping.

Work Experience Functions

CENTRAL OFFICE REPAIRER

(D.O.T. 822.281-0114)

5. Test Dial Central Office Equipment Under Super-   500
   vision of Experienced Repairer:
   a. Operate test desk to determine faults within
      an outside central office.
   b. Perform testing procedures using multitesters
      and oscilloscopes.
   c. Develop skill in detection, identification,
      isolation and finding equipment and line
      faults.

6. Repair Dial Central Office Equipment Under Super-   2000
   vision of an Experienced Repairer:

   a. Identify defective parts.
   b. Remove and replace defective parts using
      soldering gun and required hand tools.
   c. Apply relay adjustments chart information
      in final adjustment and test operate dial
      central office equipment.
   d. Requisition repair parts.
   e. Test repaired components.

7. Apply proper Troubleshooting and Safety Procedures   2000
   Related to:

   a. Electrical switching systems.
   b. Automatic switching systems.
   c. Switchboards

                                    TOTAL   8000

Schedule of Related Introduction

COURSE NUMBER	COURSE TITLE	SCHOOL	HOURS CREDIT
DD 2800/ 5900	Fundamentals of Digital Logic	MCCES	80
DF 2800/ 5900	Basic Electronics School	MCCES	B7E
DT 28xx/ 59XX	Technician Theory Course	MCCES	608.5
TF 2800	Radio Fundamentals Course	MCCES	240
TQ 2811	Telephone Switchboard Rep Cr5	MCCES	431.5
TF 2818	Teletype Repair Course	MCCES	570
TY 2827	Mobile Data Communication Terminal Technician Course	MCCES	560
TJ 2829	Mobile Communication Central Technician Course	MCCES	279
TG 2841	Ground Radio Repair Course	MCCES	7gi
TA 2851	Aviation Radio Repair Course	MCCES	476
TT 2861	Radio Technician Course	MCCES	719
TT 2866	Aviation Radio Technician Course	MCCES	457
RG 5931	Ground Radar Repair Course	MCCES	772
RG 5932	FADAC Radar Repair Course	MCCES	847
RG 5933	Artillery Electronics Repair Course	MCCES	819
RE 5934	Weapons Location Equipment Repair Course	MCCES	1059

COURSE NUMBER	COURSE TITLE	SCHOOL	HOURS CREDIT
RG 5935	Counter Mortar Radar Repair Course	MCCES/Ft. Sill	660
RH 5936	Ground Radar Technician Course	MCCES	1621
RB 5942	Aviation Radar Repairperson Course	MCCES	1316
RC 5943	Aviation Fire Control Repair Course	MCCES	835
RA 5945	Aviation Radar Repair Course (C)	MCCES	1097
RT 5947	Aviation Fire Control Technician Course	MCCES	760
RD 5948	Aviation Radar Technician Course	MCCES	1631
RJ 5962	Tactical Air Command Central Repair Course	MCCES	1194
RJ 5963	Tactical Air Operations Central Repairperson Course	MCCES	1225
RQ 5964	Tactical Data Communications Central Repairperson Course	MCCES	1578
RN 5974	Tactical Air Command Central Technician Course	MCCES	1511
RS 5977	Tactical General Purpose Computer Technician Course	MCCES	1528
RP 5978	Tactical Data Communications Computer Technician Course	MCCES	1480

INSRUCTIONS FOR COMPLETING WORK EXPERIENCE LOG

This pamphlet is issued to each registered apprentice and identifies the occupation, work process training schedules, hours allocated to each training task increment in the work process schedule and supervisory certification requirement.

1. Marine applicant will:

    a. Complete the apprentice registration application (enclosure 1) in triplicate. Forward one copy to CMC (Code OTTE), one copy placed in Marine's Service Record Book (SRB), and the third copy is to be retained by the Education Officer.

        (1) Submit the application to the commanding officer or his Authorized representative.

        (2) Obtain work experience log, which includes the Work Experience Functions. Obtain one year's supply (12 Copies) of the Apprentice Work Experience Hourly Record, (enclosure 2) from the commanding officer or education officer.

        (3) Complete the Personal History Form, (enclosure 3) and forward to CMC (Code OTTE) with enclosure (1).

        (4) Complete Military Education, (enclosure LI), and forward a certified copy t0 CMC (Code OTTE) with enclosure (1).

        (5) Complete Civilian Education, (enclosure 5), with certification from the Marine's Service Record Book and forward to CMC (Code OTTE) with enclosure (1).

        (6) Maintain Military Assignment, (enclosure 6).

        (7) Civilian Occupation, (enclosure 7), if applicable, submit statement to program sponsor on employer letterhead, giving length of employment, position held, and manner of performance.

    b. Career oriented apprentice Marines must complete the same requirements as the first-term apprentice except that they will be given credit for only half the hours required for the specific program in which they are enrolled. This is provided their previous enlistment was served in as MOS applicable to the relevant apprenticeship program for which they are applying.

(1)   A certified photocopy of enclosure (6) of the work log will be forwarded with the registration application to CMC (Code OTTE).

(2)   The Commanding Officer or his designated representative will assign credit hours for previous work experience in accordance with MCO 155C.22 and mark accordingly block 16 of enclosure (1).

2.   Procedures for recording hourly work experience

a.   Daily Record: Daily entries will be made by the apprentice.

b.   Weekly certification by supervisor: Weekly certification will be completed by the shop chief for whom the Marine works.

c.   Consolidation/Certification on Month/Yearly recapitulation: The signature line of the work experience hourly record will be signed by the commanding officer or his representative. This report will reflect the entries for the monthly work experience) enclosure (8) of work experience log.

3.   Semiannual progress interview

a.   Report to your unit Education Officer within 5 to 8 months after date of this application and twice a year thereafter. Enclosure (9) will be completed and forwarded to CMC (Code OTTE).

b.   The purpose of the interview is to determine the status of the apprentice and to certify a photocopy of the last hourly record of work experience.

c.   The Commanding Officer or Education Officer authorized representative will sign the Apprentice Progress/ Status Report (enclosure (9)).

4.   Interruption of Assignment

a.   Rifle Range/Leave. Record on the experience hourly record the days away from regular assigned duty.

b.   Separation from Active Duty. Status report will be submitted to CMC (Code OTTE) identifying the Marine as being discharged. Upon request, CMC will forward the records to Bureau of Apprenticeship and Training in the Marine's home state of record.

c. Sickness and hospitalization. Recorded by day on the Apprentice Work Experience Hourly Record.

d. Voluntary Disenrollment. An apprentice must request suspension or cancellation. Suspension retains the apprentice in a temporary status for no more than one year. A request for suspension may be mailed directly to CMC(Code OTTE) by the apprentice. Cancellation removes the apprentice from the apprenticeship program. A request for cancellation requires the signature of the apprentice's Commanding Officer of Education Officer.

5. Documentation Required to Validate Related Instruction. Certification of completion or transcript of grades will be used to award credit hours toward completion of the apprenticeship program.

6. Loss of work experience log

a. Request a reissue of a blank log from the Education Officer of your command.

b. Request CMC (Code OTTE) to furnish data available in your records to bring the log up to date.

APPRENTICE REGISTRATION APPLICATION (1500)
I-AVMC 17013 (3-77)
SN 0-09-00-006-6800 U.S. SM

1. Print or type.
2. Prepare in triplicate.
3. Forward original and one copy to CMC (Code OTTE).
4. Apprentice retains one copy in Work Experience Log.

PRIVACY ACT NOTIFICATION

Under the authority of Title 5, U.S. Code, Section 301, the information regarding your former and present active military service, educational background and present personal data is requested in order to review and evaluate your qualifications for the Department of Labor apprenticeship program for active-duty Marine Corps personnel. Your Social Security Number is used for purposes of individual identification. This information will be retained by the Commandant of the Marine Corps (Code OTTE) and by the Bureau of Apprenticeship and Training, U.S. Department of Labor, and will not be divulged without your written authorization to anyone other than Headquarters Marine Corps and Department of Labor personnel involved with administration of this program. You are not required to provide this information; however, failure to do so may result in your not being registered for an apprenticeable trade.

APPLICANT INFORMATION

1. NAME (last, first, middle)	2. SSN	3. DATE OF BIRTH (Day, Month, Year)	4. SEX ☐ MALE ☐ FEMALE

5. RACE ETHNIC GROUP
☐ CAUCASIAN/ WHITE ☐ NEGRO BLACK ☐ AMERICAN INDIAN ☐ SPANISH AMERICAN ☐ ORIENTAL ☐ INFORMATION NOT AVAILABLE ☐ NOT ELSEWHERE CLASSIFIED

6. NAME AND LOCATION OF HIGH SCHOOL FROM WHICH GRADUATED   OR, STATE AND DATE OF GED EQUIVALENCY

7. Did you serve on active duty on or after 5 August 1964 and before 8 May, 1975? ☐ YES ☐ NO	8. HOME OF RECORD (State)

9. APPRENTICEABLE TRADE FOR REGISTRATION (Give complete title)	10. DOT CODE FOR APPRENTICEABLE TRADE	11. APPRENTICE PROGRAM

I agree to report to the education officer within 5 to 8 months after date of this application and twice a year thereafter. I understand that my registration is voluntary and that registration does not guarantee work or duty assignments appropriate to my apprenticeship. I have read and understand the Privacy Act Statement.

12. Signature of applicant _____   13. Date _____

TO BE FILLED IN BY APPLICANT'S COMMANDING OFFICER OR EDUCATION OFFICER

TO: Commandant of the Marine Corps (Code OTTE), Headquarters U.S. Marine Corps, Washington, D.C. 20380

14. FROM

15. Total hours required for term of apprenticeship _____ hours

16. Hours credit given for previous work experience (-) _____ hours

17. Total hours remaining for term of apprenticeship _____ hours

18. COMMENTS (If any)

19. SIGNATURE OF REGISTRAR The applicant has been counseled as to the conditions and requirements of the apprenticeship. Signature _____	20. TITLE	21. DATE

Enclosure (1)

INSTRUCTIONS FOR APPRENTICE REGISTRATION APPLICATION

Item No.   \

   1.   Self-explanatory.
   2.   Enter Social Security Number. Example: 399-03-6433
   3.   Enter date of birth: Day, Month, Year.
   4.   Self-explanatory.
   5.   Self-explanatory
   6.   Self-explanatory.
   7.   A check X in the YES block signifies that the registrant is
regarded as a Viet Nam veteran by the Department of Labor.
   8.   Enter name of state which the registrant calls home.
   9.   Enter long title of apprenticeable trade. Example: Camera
Repairer. Entries are limited to those apprenticeships authorized by the
Commandant of the Marine Corps.
   10. Enter 9-digit DOT code which matches the apprenticeable trade
entered in Item 9. The Work Processes Schedule indicates this code.
   11. No entry required.
   12. Self-explanatory.
   13. Self-explanatory.
   14. Enter name and address of command forwarding application.
   15. Enter total term of the apprenticeship (required hours for
completion). Example: 6000. The Work Processes Schedule indicates the
total term of the apprenticeship.
   16. Enter hours of creditable work experience completed prior to
registration, if any. Registrant may be credited with 1000 hours of
previous work experience for each full year that his/her service record
validates assignment to an MOS applicable to the apprenticeable
trade. Applicable MOSs, if any, are listed at the bottom of the Work
Processes Schedule for each authorized apprenticeable trade. However,
credit for previous work experience completed prior to registration cannot
exceed more than 50% of the term of the apprenticeship. Therefore, no
more than 3000 hours of previous work experience can be credited to a
6000-hour apprenticeship. Portions or fractions of years of work
experience will not be credited.
   17. Enter the difference between Item 15 and Item 16. This difference
is the number of work experience hours which must be completed by the
apprentice.
   18. Enter any comments regarding previous work experience, future
assignment or next duty, or further explanation of any above item. Entry
not mandatory.
   19. Signature of co-ending officer1 education officer, or his authorized
representative.
   20. Title of registrar who signed Item 19.
   21. Enter date that Item 19 was signed. This will be the effective
beginning date of the apprenticeship.

Enclosure (1)

17

APPRENTICE WORK EXPERIENCE HOURLY RECORD (1500)
NAVMC 11015 (3-77)
SN: 0000-00-005-6840 U/I: SH

APPRENTICE NAME (Last, first, middle)

1. Print legibly.
2. Enter completed hours daily or weekly.
3. Have Supervisor verify hours at the end of each week.
4. Keep this record in your Work Experience Log.

WEEK OF	DATE FROM						DATE TO						SIGNATURE & TITLE OF SUPERVISOR														

DAY	LETTERS IDENTIFIED IN WORK PROCESSES SCHEDULE																										TOTAL HOURS
	A	B	C	D	E	F	G	H	I	J	K	L	M	N	O	P	Q	R	S	T	U	V	W	X	Y	Z	
SUN																											
MON																											
TUES																											
WED																											
THURS																											
FRI																											
SAT																											
TOTAL HOURS																											

WEEK OF	DATE FROM						DATE TO						SIGNATURE & TITLE OF SUPERVISOR														

DAY	LETTERS IDENTIFIED IN WORK PROCESSES SCHEDULE																										TOTAL HOURS
	A	B	C	D	E	F	G	H	I	J	K	L	M	N	O	P	Q	R	S	T	U	V	W	X	Y	Z	
SUN																											
MON																											
TUES																											
WED																											
THURS																											
FRI																											
SAT																											
TOTAL HOURS																											

WEEK OF	DATE FROM						DATE TO						SIGNATURE & TITLE OF SUPERVISOR														

DAY	LETTERS IDENTIFIED IN WORK PROCESSES SCHEDULE																										TOTAL HOURS
	A	B	C	D	E	F	G	H	I	J	K	L	M	N	O	P	Q	R	S	T	U	V	W	X	Y	Z	
SUN																											
MON																											
TUES																											
WED																											
THURS																											
FRI																											
SAT																											
TOTAL HOURS																											

Enclosure (2)

WEEK OF	DATE FROM					DATE TO					SIGNATURE & TITLE OF SUPERVISOR															
DAY	LETTERS IDENTIFIED IN WORK PROCESSES SCHEDULE																									TOTAL HOURS
	A	B	C	D	E	F	G	H	I	J	K	L	M	N	O	P	Q	R	S	T	U	V	W	X	Y	Z	
SUN																											
MON																											
TUES																											
WED																											
THURS																											
FRI																											
SAT																											
TOTAL HOURS																											

WEEK OF	DATE FROM					DATE TO					SIGNATURE & TITLE OF SUPERVISOR															
DAY	LETTERS IDENTIFIED IN WORK PROCESSES SCHEDULE																									TOTAL HOURS
	A	B	C	D	E	F	G	H	I	J	K	L	M	N	O	P	Q	R	S	T	U	V	W	X	Y	Z	
SUN																											
MON																											
TUES																											
WED																											
THURS																											
FRI																											
SAT																											
TOTAL HOURS																											

SIGNATURE & TITLE	DATE

Enclosure (2)

PERSONAL HISTORY

LAST NAME	FIRST NAME	MIDDLE INT.
RANK	SOCIAL SECURITY NUMBER	DATE OF BIRTH DAY/MONTH/YEAR

PLACE OF BIRTH

PERMANENT HOME OF RECORD

SIGNATURE OF APPRENTICE   DATE

_____   _____

MILITARY EDUCATION

COURSE TITLE	LOCATION	LENGTH;	FROM:	TO:

TOTAL EDUCUCATION HOURS_____	FIRST YEAR HRS._____	SECOND YEAR HRS._____	THIRD YEAR HRS._____
	CERTIFIED: _____	CERTIFIED: _____	CERTIFIED: _____

Enclosure (4)

CIVILIAN EDUCATION

HIGH SCHOOL OR GED/ NAME, ADDRESS, ZIP CODE/ GRAD. DATE

COLLEGE OR GED/ NAME, ADDRESS, ZIP CODE/ GRAD. DATE

VOCATIONAL SCHOOLS

LIST ALL SEPARATE COURSES TAKEN

LIST ALL OTHER SPECIALIZED TRAINING NOT COVERED ABOVE

Enclosure (5)

MILITARY ASSIGNMENT

UNIT	ADDRESS	FROM	TO	DUTY ASSIGNMENT

Enclosure (6)

LIST ALL CENTRAL OFFICE REPAIRER RELATED EMPLOYMENT COVERING THE LAST TEN (10) YEARS.		
FIRM, NAME AND ADDRESS	NO. OF YEARS	POSITION HELD

Enclosure (7)

WORK EXPERIENCE

	Jan	Feb	Mar	Apr	May	Jun	Jul	Aug	Sep	Oct	Nov	Dec	Total For Yr	Int
A														
B														
C														
D														
E														
F														
G														
H														
I														
J														
K														
L														
M														
N														
O														
P														
Q														
R														
S														
T														
U														
V														

A. TOOLS
B. MATERIALS
C. SYSTEMS TERMINOLOGY
D. DISTRIBUTING FRAMES
E. SHIP CLEANING TECHNIQUES
F. SAFETY PRACTICES
G. MAINTEANCE ADMINISTRATION
H. TELEPHONE SWITCHING
I. ELECTRICAL STEPPING SWITCHES
J. LINE CONDITIONING EQUIPMENT
K. INTERCEPT EQUIPMENT

L. AUTOVON TRUCK CIRCUIT EQUIPMENT
M. INSTALLATION PRACTICES
N. CABLE COLOR CODES
O. WIRE WRAPPING
P. TESTING PROCEDURES
Q. TROUBLESHOOTING
R. SOLDERING GUN/HAND TOOLS
S. REQUISITIONING
T. ELECTRICAL SWITCHING SYSTEMS
U. AUTOMATIC SWITCHING SYSTEMS
V. SWITCHBOARDS

_____
CERTIFICATION OFFICIAL

_____
TITLE

Enclosure (8)

APPRENTICE PROGRESS/STATUS REPORT (1500)

APPRENTICE PROGRESS/STATUS REPORT (1500)
NAVMC 11014 (3-77)
SN: 0000-00-006-6840 U/I: SH

1. Print or type.
2. Prepare in triplicate.
3. Forward original and one copy to CMC (Code OTTE) with attached photo of last Hourly Record of Work Experience.
4. Apprentice retains one copy in Work Experience Log.

PRIVACY ACT NOTIFICATION

Under the authority of Title S, U.S. Code, Section 301, the information regarding your former and present military service, educational background and present personal data is requested for purposes of individual identification. This information will be retained by the Commandant of the Marine Corps (Code OTTE) and by the Bureau of Apprenticeship and Training, U.S. Department of Labor and will not be divulged without your written authorization to anyone other than Headquarters Marine Corps and Department of Labor personnel involved with the administration of the apprenticeship program. You are not required to provide this information; however, failure to do so may result in cancellation of your registration in an apprenticeable trade.

To be filled in by Apprentice or official in accordance with instructions on reverse side.

1. NAME OF APPRENTICE (Last, first, middle)	2. SSN	3. SEX ☐ MALE ☐ FEMALE

4. RACE/ETHNIC GROUP
☐ CAUCASIAN/WHITE   ☐ NEGRO/BLACK   ☐ AMERICAN INDIAN   ☐ SPANISH AMERICAN   ☐ ORIENTAL   ☐ INFORMATION NOT AVAILABLE   ☐ NOT ELSEWHERE CLASSIFIED

5. Did you serve on active duty on or after 5 August 1964 and before 8 May 1975? ☐ YES ☐ NO	6. HOME OF RECORD (State)

7. Apprenticeable Trade in Which Registered	8. Total Hours for Term	9. Hrs. Preregistration Experience	10. Hrs. Completed Since Registration	11. Hours Remaining

TO: Commandant of the Marine Corps (Code OTTE), Headquarters U.S. Marine Corps, Washington, D.C. 20380

12. FROM (Activity submitting report)

ACTION REQUESTED
(check one)

13. Please suspend registration for the apprentice named above for the reason(s) checked below:

a. ☐ Orders to light duty

b. ☐ Nature of current assignment prohibits work in apprenticeable trade for one year or less

c. ☐ Hospitalization

d. ☐ Operational commitments prevent reporting for progress interview

14. ☐ Please lift the suspension of registration for the apprentice named above effective: _____
(Date)

15. ☐ Please cancel the registration of the apprentice named above for the reason(s) checked below:

a. ☐ Commanding officer's prerogative

b. ☐ Discharge or release to inactive duty

c. ☐ Termination of work experience for one year or more

d. ☐ Death

e. ☐ Failure to report for twice-a-year apprentice progress interview

f. ☐ Personal request of apprentice

16. ☐ The apprentice named above has completed all required hours of work experience in all areas of the apprentice trade. A "Certificate of Apprenticeship Completion" is requested.

17. SIGNATURE OF APPRENTICE	18. DATE

19. SIGNATURE AND TITLE OF OFFICIAL	20. DATE

Enclosure (9)

INSTRUCTIONS FOR APPRENTICE PROGRESS/STATUS REPORT

Item No.

1. Self-explanatory.
2. Enter Social Security Number. Example: 399.03-6433.
3. Self-explanatory.
4. Self-explanatory. Must agree with Item 5 of apprentice registration.
5. Entry must agree with Item 7 of apprentice registration.
6. Enter name of state which the apprentice calls home.
7. Enter long title of apprenticeable trade. Example: Camera Repairer.

ITEMS 8.9,10, and 11 NOT REQUIRED IF SUSPENSION (Item 13) OR CANCELLATION (Item 15) IS REQUESTED.

8. Enter total term of apprenticeship as indicated on Work Processes Schedule. Must agree with Item 15 of "Apprentice Registration Application."
9. Enter number of verified hours of work experience completed prior to registration. Must agree with Item 16 of "Apprentice Registration Application."
10. Enter cumulative number of hours of work experience completed as a registered apprentice. Attach reproduced copy (photostat or xerox) of every "Work Experience Hourly Record" which snows hours completed since lest report.
11. Add Item 9and Item 10 and subtract total from Item 8. Enter result in Item 11.
12. Name and address of activity from which report is submitted.
13. Check if this is a request for suspension. Suspension retains the apprentice in a temporary inactive status for no more than one year. Request for suspension requires signature of apprentice in Item 17. A request for a suspension may be mailed directly to Commandant of the Marine Corps by apprentice. No suspension will be carried longer than one year.
14. Check here if reason for suspension longer applies. A request for suspension requires signature of apprentice in Item 17 and signature of Commanding Officer or Education Officer in Item 19.
15. Check here is this is a request for cancellation. Cancellation removes the apprentice from the apprenticeship program. A request for cancellation requires signature of Commanding Officer or Education Officer in Item 19.
16. Check if apprentice has completed all required work experience, both grand total of hours and total hours in each skill area. A check in this block must be supported by final entries in Items 8,9.10 and 11, plus a produced copy of the "Work Experience Hourly Record" completed since the last apprentice progress interview or report. Hours of verified work experience completed before registration (Item 9), if any, will be distributed equally among the skill area of the trade. A check in this block requires signatures in Item 17 and Item 19.
17. Signature of apprentice required for Items 8,9, 10,11.13, 14, 15f and 16.
18. Date in which signature of apprentice is affixed in Item 17.
19. Signature of commanding officer or education officer submitting report required for Items 8, 9,10,11, 13, 14, 15 and 15f.
20. Date on which signature in Item 19 is affixed.

Enclosure (9)

Certificate of Completion of Apprenticeship

United States Department of Labor

Bureau of Apprenticeship and Training

This is to certify that

has completed an apprenticeship in the trade of

in compliance with the standards recommended by the Federal Committee on Apprenticeship.

SAMPLE

William D. Kelling
SECRETARY OF LABOR

Hugh C. Murphy
BUREAU ADMINISTRATOR

www.ingramcontent.com/pod-product-compliance
Lightning Source LLC
Chambersburg PA
CBHW080936290526
45795CB00007BA/2776